Eternity

How to KNOW where you will spend eternity

Jim Clark

Published by

J. Charles Clark Publishing
a division of J. Charles Clark Consulting, Inc.
a member of the Clark Group of American Companies

ISBN 978-0-692-82675-1

Published in the United States of America

1st Edition - 2023

Confirmation of Doctrinal Accuracy

The doctrine set forth herein is solid. It is based on God's Holy Word, the Bible. May it be an encouragement to your heart and a guide to your salvation. Our special thanks to Dr. Sloan for taking his time to vet the manuscript for accuracy.

> "*Mr. Clark, I have reviewed your document and it is very well done. The doctrine is sound. May many come to know Jesus as their Savior as a result of reading it.*"

Daniel Sloan , Ph.D.
Adjunct Professor of Biblical Studies
LUO Program Director for MA in Biblical Studies
and MA in Biblical Exposition
John W. Rawlings School of Divinity
Liberty University

Special Dedications

This book is dedicated to my Lord and Savior Jesus, who gave His life on the Cross to pay for my sins so that I might live. Thank you, Lord Jesus. Praise God.

This book is also dedicated to my Aunt Reba, who loved her little Jimmy enough to send him to church camp where he met his Savior, Jesus. Thank you, Aunt Reba.

Table of Contents

Prologue

The purpose of this book is to explain how you can KNOW where you will spend eternity.

IF you drop dead this very minute, while you are reading this book, WHERE will you spend eternity? Of the millions of questions we answer during our lives, this is the Number One most important question we will ever answer. No other question is as important, yet the vast majority of people never answer it. What about you? Have you dealt with this question?

There are only two places to go when you die, Heaven and Hell.

Heaven is where God lives. It's a place filled with the love and beauty of God. There is no grief, no sorrow, no pain, and no suffering. There is only the joy and peace of being in God's presence as you experience the love and beauty of God.

Hell is where Satan will live. It's a place of indescribable pain and suffering and it is FOREVER.

Once you arrive, you can NEVER leave. You are in constant pain and suffering for eternity.

God wants you to spend eternity with Him in Heaven. Satan wants you to spend eternity with him in Hell. The following chapters explain how to do both. YOU will decide what you will do.

John 3:16

"For God so loved the world, that he gave his only Son,
that whoever believes in him should not perish
but have eternal life."

Good and Evil

There is only ONE real God, He is God Jehovah of the Bible. All other gods are false, they are Satan in disguise.

God is PURE GOOD. There is no evil in Him.

God loves you. He loves you more than words can describe. He wants what's best for you. He wants you to be with Him in Heaven. He has done everything that can be done to make it possible for you to spend eternity with Him, up to and including sending His Son Jesus to die on the Cross to pay for your sins.

Jesus is God's Son. He is EVERYTHING. He is PERFECTION. He is the embodiment of God because His love is total and complete. He is our Savior, He is our Protector, and He is our Example. Without Jesus, we HAVE nothing, we ARE nothing.

Satan is PURE EVIL. There is no good in him.

Satan was an angel in Heaven. He wanted to be God and take His place in Heaven so he started a fight with God. God won. He threw Satan and his buddies out of Heaven. Since then, Satan has been trying to get even with God. He can't whip God, so he tries to hurt God by hurting God's children, you and me.

Get this, if you don't get anything else. Satan hates your guts. He is a dirty, filthy, stinking, disgusting, greasy, EVIL creature who wants to destroy you. He is a vicious animal who will rip you apart and laugh while he's doing it. When you die he wants you to spend the rest of eternity in Hell being tortured in a burning lake of fire. Until you die he wants you to live a miserable life. That's what Satan wants for you.

John 3:16

*"For God so loved the world, that he gave his only Son,
that whoever believes in him should not perish
but have eternal life."*

Good and Evil

Hell is real. It is a horrible place of torment and torture. Those who go to Hell burn in a literal lake of fire. Ever burn your finger on a hot stove? How about burning your whole body like that, with one very big exception. When you burn your finger you know it will stop hurting after a while. When you are in Hell your entire body will burn. It will hurt just like your finger hurt, but it will never stop. You will burn forever.

Hell is the automatic, it is the default destination. You don't have to do anything to go to Hell. If you do nothing, you will wake up in Hell when you die and that is where you will suffer for eternity. If you want to go to Heaven when you die, you must DO something. You must be SAVED.

Revelation 20:15

"And whosoever was not found written in the book of life was cast into the lake of fire."

John 3:16

“For God so loved the world, that he gave his only Son,
that whoever believes in him should not perish
but have eternal life.”

SAVED

The Bible says everyone has sinned, including you. It says the penalty for sinning is death, meaning eternal punishment in Hell.

The Bible says there is nothing you can do to make up for the sins you have done. It says the best thing you ever did was like a dirty rag in God's eyes. He just is not impressed by what man does.

Your sins must be paid for. Someone must pay for your sins. Since you can't do it God sent His son Jesus to do it for you. When Jesus shed his blood on the Cross your sins were paid for with His blood. Your Sin Debt was marked PAID IN FULL. That's why Jesus is called Savior. When He died on the Cross for you, He SAVED you from an eternity of torture and torment in Hell.

Don't think you need a savior because you've lived a good life? Be careful with that. Don't be fooled. That is exactly what the "Father of Lies" Satan wants you to believe. Remember, God is not impressed with man's good deeds. Your living a good life means nothing to Him if you reject the price His Son Jesus paid on the Cross for you.

Romans 3:23-26

"For all have sinned, and come short of the glory of God."

Isaiah 64:6

"But we are all as an unclean thing, and all our righteousnesses are as filthy rags."

Romans 6:23

"For the wages of sin is death; but the gift of God is eternal life through Jesus Christ our Lord."

John 3:16

*"For God so loved the world, that he gave his only Son,
that whoever believes in him should not perish
but have eternal life."*

Steps to Salvation

There are five simple steps to being saved.

1. Recognize and admit that you have sinned.

2. Recognize and admit that there is nothing you can do to pay for your sins, that you need a savior.

3. Recognize and believe that Jesus paid for your sins with His shed blood on the Cross, HE is your Savior.

4. Ask God to forgive you for your sins and accept His gift of eternal life through Jesus' shed blood on the Cross.

5. Thank God and praise Him for His mercy and love.

Bow your head. Bow your head now and pray this simple prayer:

> *"God, I know I have sinned. I know there is nothing I can do to make up for the sins I have committed. I believe Jesus shed His blood on the Cross to pay for my sins. God, please forgive me for my sins. I accept your gift of eternal life through Jesus' shed blood on the Cross. Thank you, God, for your mercy and love."*

The split second you pray this prayer your sins will be forgiven and God's angels will rejoice and God will write your name in the Lamb's Book of Life (God's reservation book for Heaven). You will have a NEW BEGINNING. Your Bible will be your instruction manual for how you are to live your new life.

John 3:16

"For God so loved the world, that he gave his only Son,
that whoever believes in him should not perish
but have eternal life."

Read your Bible and you'll know what to do and what not to do. Don't depend on what feels right. The Bible says the ways of a man seem right to him. Don't depend on what someone else, even a preacher, tells you. Read your Bible and listen to God as He speaks to you through His word. Then you'll know how God expects you to live your life.

Proverbs 21:2

"Every way of man is right in his own eyes…"

John 3:16

"For God so loved the world, that he gave his only Son,
that whoever believes in him should not perish
but have eternal life."

License to Sin

Now that you're saved and your name is written in the Lamb's Book of Life you can live any way you want to, right? WRONG. God makes it very clear that He expects you to live a godly life. He has rules and He expects you to follow them. If you don't you will not "inherit the kingdom of God" when you die, you will inherit Hell, the kingdom of Satan.

What about those who say that once a person has accepted Jesus and has been saved it is impossible for him to go to Hell? They need to read their Bibles. "Know ye not that the unrighteous shall not inherit the kingdom of God?" is about as plain as it can be. It doesn't say, "Know ye not that the unrighteous shall not inherit the kingdom of God, UNLESS they have been saved, in which case they can live any way they want to live." Does it? No, it does not. Live a godless life and you will not go to Heaven when you die, you will go straight to Hell. Period.

Are there any exceptions? Yes. REPENTENCE. If you get on the wrong track after you are saved and you repent, God is faithful to forgive. How many times can you commit the same sins and be forgiven? That's between you and God. Personally, I wouldn't push it.

Just because you receive a gift, that does not mean you have to keep it. You can always give it back. The same goes for eternal salvation. Just because you accept God's gift of eternal life through Jesus' shed blood on the Cross, that does not mean you have to keep it. All you have to do to give it back is turn your back on God and live a godless life. God doesn't force anyone to join Him in Heaven, God doesn't beg anyone to join Him in Heaven, nor does God let those who live a godless life live with Him in Heaven. That would defeat the purpose of Heaven, wouldn't it?

John 3:16

"For God so loved the world, that he gave his only Son,
that whoever believes in him should not perish
but have eternal life."

License to Sin

1 John 1:9

"If we confess our sins, He is faithful and just to forgive us our sins, and to cleanse us from all unrighteousness."

1 Corinthians 6:9 and 6:10.

"Know ye not that the unrighteous shall not inherit the kingdom of God? Be not deceived: neither fornicators, nor idolaters, nor adulterers, nor effeminate, nor abusers of themselves with mankind, (10) Nor thieves, nor covetous, nor drunkards, nor revilers, nor extortioners, shall inherit the kingdom of God."

Galatians 5:19

"Now the works of the flesh are manifest, which are these: adultery, fornication, uncleanness, lasciviousness, idolatry, witchcraft, hatred, variance, emulations, wrath, strife, seditions, heresies, envyings, murders, drunkenness, revellings, and such like: of the which I tell you before, as I have also told you in time past, that they which do such things shall not inherit the kingdom of God."

John 3:16

"For God so loved the world, that he gave his only Son, that whoever believes in him should not perish but have eternal life."

A Better Life Now

WHERE is Satan now? Is he in Hell? No, he is not. He is down here on the ground with us.

One day God asked Satan where he had been. Satan answered and told God that he "had been going to and fro in the earth, and from walking up and down in it". Satan was NOT walking to and fro in the earth looking for an ice cream cone. He was walking to and fro in the earth looking for YOU, so he could destroy your life.

Satan has a three-fold plan to destroy you.

1. First, he wants to steal your soul. He wants to keep you so busy that you don't get around to dealing with where you will spend eternity. He knows that if he can do that long enough, you will wake up one day and find yourself in Hell, forever.

2. Second, if he can't steal your soul because you get saved, he wants to steal your testimony. He wants to make your life so miserable that no one else will want to get saved to have what you have. WHO wants to get saved and have a miserable life like you? If Satan can't steal your soul he wants to steal your ability to demonstrate what a wonderful and peaceful life a person can have in Jesus.

3. Third, he wants to steal your joy. There is joy in being saved. There is the peace that only comes from knowing Jesus as your Savior. After sinning with Bathsheba, King David prayed for forgiveness and asked God to "restore unto me the joy of thy salvation". Remember, Satan hates your guts. He does NOT want you to be happy. He does not want you to have peace in your heart and mind. He wants you to be miserable,

John 3:16

“For God so loved the world, that he gave his only Son,
that whoever believes in him should not perish
but have eternal life.”

hopefully so miserable that you even commit suicide. THAT is how much Satan hates you. Believe it

Satan roams the earth tearing down and destroying lives. He is good at what he does. If you aren't saved you are ON YOUR OWN, and you will lose the attacks Satan levels at you. You are just not up to it. You are just not powerful enough to fight Satan on your own and win. No one is. If you try to do battle with Satan alone, you will lose. Period. Your life will be destroyed and you will end up in Hell when you die.

Thankfully for you and me, God has a plan too. The split second you accept Jesus as your Savior, God will send His Holy Spirit to live in your heart. The Holy Spirit is a real person. His job is to guide you and protect you while you are still on this earth. He is with you every second of every day and He is on guard.

When Satan whispers in your ear and tells you to do something ungodly. the Holy Spirit will whisper in your other ear and suggest that you don't do what Satan is suggesting. He will SUGGEST that you don't do what Satan is suggesting. You have free will, you will make the decision.

When Satan creates circumstances in your life that make you sad, or nervous, or afraid, the Holy Spirit will whisper in your ear a Bible verse that will remind you that God is with you. For example, when you are worried about something the Holy Spirit will whisper "For God hath not given us the spirit of fear, but of power, and of love, and of a sound mind." That will remind you that the fear and worry that you are experiencing is from Satan, not God. Then the Holy Spirit will whisper "And the peace of God,

John 3:16

*"For God so loved the world, that he gave his only Son,
that whoever believes in him should not perish
but have eternal life."*

which passeth all understanding, shall keep your hearts and minds through Christ Jesus." That will remind you to say a little prayer and ask God for His peace in your heart. The SPLIT SECOND you ask, God will fill your heart with so much joy you will feel like you are going to explode from happiness. The tears will run down your cheeks and you will praise God for His love. That is when Satan will move on to someone else because he will know that he has lost that attack on you. You must be wise enough not to get cocky. Satan will come back, but when he does he'll find the Holy Spirit is still with you. Praise God.

Read your Bible and memorize verses. Then, the Holy Spirit will remind you of the verse you need when you need it. What a wonderful blessing from God is His Holy Spirit. Thank you, Lord.

Job 1:7

"And the LORD said unto Satan, Whence comest thou?
Then Satan answered the LORD, and said,
From going to and fro in the earth, and from
walking up and down in it."

Philippians 4:7

"And the peace of God, which passeth all understanding,
shall keep your hearts and minds through Christ Jesus."

2 Timothy 1:7

"For God hath not given us the spirit of fear; but of power,
and of love, and of a sound mind."

Psalms 51:12

"Restore unto me the joy of thy salvation; and
uphold me with thy free spirit."

John 3:16

"For God so loved the world, that he gave his only Son,
that whoever believes in him should not perish
but have eternal life."

Epilogue

So now you know the truth. It's up to you to decide where and with whom you will spend eternity.

You can accept God's gift of eternal life through Jesus' shed blood on the Cross and spend eternity with Him in Heaven, or you can do nothing and wake up one day with Satan in Hell. You can live a life before you die that is filled with joy and peace, or you can go through life alone filled with worry, stress, and pain.

It's YOUR decision but remember one thing. Ignoring Hell doesn't make it go away, any more than ignoring a severed arm stops the bleeding. Ignore a severed arm and you'll bleed to death. Ignore Hell and that's where you'll spend eternity.

Don't ignore Hell. Deal with it. Deal with it NOW, before it's too late. Bow your head, repent, and accept God's gift of eternal life through Jesus. Then show God how much you appreciate His gift by living a godly life.

> *"God, I know I have sinned. I know there is nothing I can do to make up for the sins I have committed. I believe Jesus shed His blood on the Cross to pay for my sins. God, please forgive me for my sins. I accept your gift of eternal life through Jesus' shed blood on the Cross. Thank you, God, for your mercy and love."*

Index

Jim Clark Ministries™

Jim Clark Ministries™ is an exciting ministry with a specific purpose, to share the gospel of Jesus Christ.

The primary tool used to share the gospel of Jesus is Jim Clark's outstanding book: "Eternity - How to KNOW where you will spend eternity". The ministry's mission is to distribute 1 million copies per year, then, 1 billion.

Jim Clark Ministries™ does not accept cash donations. All expenses are paid by Jim Clark or one of his companies. If you wish to help, you may buy copies of Eternity and distribute them to your family, friends, and strangers. If you prefer, Jim Clark Ministries™ will distribute the copies you donate.

Jim Clark books are J. Charles Clark Publishing publications.This and other outstanding books by the author may be purchased at:

www.jimclarkbooks.com

Jim Clark Ministries™

Praising and Serving
God, Jesus, and the Holy Spirit™

Jim Clark is an award-winning internationally-published author. He is the recipient of the International Poetry Society's coveted Editor's Choice Award for his outstanding book of romantic poems:

May I Dream?

A collection of poems on matters of the heart.

Jim Clark Books

Jim Clark books are exciting. There are four genres: Retirement Planning, Romance, Life on Earth, and Textbooks. Regardless of whether you're feeling romantic, planning your retirement, protecting your estate, or preparing for a new career, you'll find the right book in Jim Clark's outstanding collection.

Jim Clark books carry a three-fold purpose: to inform, to entertain, and to raise awareness that there are children in America who go to bed hungry. Profits from Jim Clark's books are donated to feeding hungry American children.

Jim Clark books are J. Charles Clark Publishing publications. This and other outstanding books by the author may be purchased at:

www.jimclarkbooks.com

To learn how you can help feed every hungry child in America visit

jimclarkamerican.com/children.

Made in the USA
Monee, IL
04 November 2026

67385513R00022